When I'm At Work

Recycling Operative

Written by Sue Barraclough
Photography by Chris Fairclough

FRANKLIN WATTS
LONDON • SYDNEY

First published in 2006 by Franklin Watts
338 Euston Road, London NW1 3BH

Franklin Watts Australia
Hachette Children's Books
Level 17/207 Kent Street
Sydney NSW 2000

Editor: Adrian Cole
Designer: Jemima Lumley
Art direction: Jonathan Hair
Photography: Chris Fairclough, except page 28bcr

The publisher wishes to thank Tanya, Danny, Giovanni and Greg
at ECT Recycling. Thanks also to Kira and Christopher for taking
part, and the pupils of Sea Mills Infant School, Bristol.
© Digital Vision Ltd. All rights reserved page 28bcr.

A CIP catalogue record for this book is available from the
British Library

ISBN 0 7496 6391 X

Printed in China

Contents

I am a recycling operative

My name is Tanya. My job is to collect materials such as metal, paper and glass to be recycled.

Recycled materials are used again and not just thrown away.

I work with another operative called Danny.

My bright waistcoat makes sure I will be seen while I am working.

Starting work

We start work early.
I look at the map to
check the round.

I take out some new
recycling boxes to the
truck. I will need to
deliver these later on.

Now we are ready to set off.

Collecting boxes

People fill up their black boxes with things to be recycled. They leave the boxes outside their homes for us to collect.

It helps us when people sort things into different groups in the box.

Emptying boxes

First, we hook the boxes on to the side of the
truck. Then we sort each type of material
into different compartments in the truck.

Sorting recycling is noisy work and the glass sometimes smashes. I have ear plugs for my ears, and goggles to protect my eyes.

Driving and delivering

Danny walks ahead to get the next group of boxes ready. I drive along the road to meet up with him.

I deliver one of
the new recycling
boxes.

I also post a letter
about recycling
and collections.

Collecting from schools

We also pick up recycling boxes and bags of paper from schools.

In the schools, the children collect their scrap paper in a box in the classroom. On collection day, the box is left out for us to pick up.

Filling the truck

We keep
unloading
boxes and
sorting
materials.
The truck fills
up with cans,
glass, paper
and batteries.

Once the truck is full we drive back
to the depot. At the gatehouse, I
drive the truck on to some huge
scales to be weighed.

Back at the depot

First, we unload any clothes, engine oil and batteries.

Then we hand the truck over to the fork-lift drivers to unload.

The fork-lift truck driver lifts out the container of paper and adds it to a huge pile.

Unloading and sorting

The metal tins and cans are unloaded. They are tipped on to one heap.

Then the glass bottles are tipped on to another heap.

Huge heaps of different materials build up during the day.

Finishing work

By the afternoon we have finished collecting. Everything is unloaded and sorted, ready to be transported to recycling factories.

All the trucks are parked in a line,
ready to start work again tomorrow.

Recycling equipment

This **recycling box** is made to hang on hooks on the side of the truck. This makes it easier to sort the materials.

This **waistcoat** is bright yellow with reflective strips. It means that car drivers will notice the recycling operative while she collects boxes.

These **goggles** protect eyes from dust, dirt and splinters of glass.

The recycling operative wears thick waterproof **gloves** to protect her hands from spills and sharp objects while she works.

These **ear plugs** block out the noise of the glass smashing and cans crashing.

Recycle and reduce waste

• Find out what materials your local recycling team collects.

• Take other materials to recycling centres or collection banks.

• Make compost with kitchen waste.

Metal is melted and made into new cans.

Batteries are made safe and then recycled.

Glass is melted and made into new bottles.

Paper is made into new paper products.

How you can help:

Ask an adult to wash out bottles and cans.

⬇

Put different materials in separate bags or bundles, so it is easier to sort.

⬇

Leave the box outside your home on the right day.

Glossary and index

Compartments - different sections into which things can be put. For example, different materials are sorted into separate compartments on a recycling truck. **Page 12.**

Depot - a place where things are stored. **Page 19.**

Equipment - things you need to do a task. **Pages 26-27.**

Materials - glass, plastic, metal and paper are all types of material. **Pages 6, 11, 12, 18, 23, 28, 29.**

Recycling - using materials again to make something else. **Pages 13, 15.**

Recycling boxes - strong, plastic boxes used by people to store things for recycling. **Pages 8, 11, 12, 14-16, 26.**

Recycling collections - the times when recycling boxes are collected and emptied. **Pages 15, 17.**

Scales - a machine used to measure weight: how heavy or light something is. **Page 19.**